SOCIAL IMPERIALISM

WITH AN EXCERPT FROM
Imperialism,
The Highest Stage of Capitalism
BY V. I. LENIN

By

JOHN
ATKINSON HOBSON

First published in 1920

British Library Cataloguing-in-Publication Data
A catalogue record for this book is available
from the British Library

THE HIGHEST
STAGE OF CAPITALISM

AN EXCERPT FROM
Imperialism, The Highest Stage Of Capitalism
BY V. I. LENIN

During the past fifteen or twenty years, especially after the Spanish-American War (1898) and the Anglo-Boer War (1899-1902), the economic and also the political literature of the old and new world has more and more often adopted the term "imperialism" in order to characterise the epoch in which we live. In 1902, *Imperialism*, a work by English economist, J. A. Hobson, was published in London and New York. The author, who adopts the point of view of bourgeois social reformism and pacifism, which in essence is identical with the present position of the ex-Marxist, K. Kautsky, gives a very good and detailed description of the principal economic and political characteristics of imperialism.... Hobson, in his work on imperialism, marks the years 1884-1900 as being the period of intensified "expansion" of the chief European states. According to his estimate, England during these years acquired 3.7 million square miles of territory with a population of 57 million ; France acquired 3.6 million ; Germany one million square miles with 16.7 million inhabitants ; Belgium 900,000 square miles with 30 million inhabitants ; Portugal 800,000 square miles with 9 million inhabitants. The quest for colonies by all capitalist states at the end of the nineteenth century, and particularly since the 1880's, is a well-known fact in the history of diplomacy and of foreign policy.

SOCIALISTIC IMPERIALISM

SOCIALISTIC IMPERIALISM.

I.

Some liberals with socialistic leanings and a few professed socialists support the South African war and the Imperialism it embodies by two arguments which deserve attention. The first runs as follows: If an individual member of society, owning land, neglects to develop its natural resources or so uses it as to make it a public nuisance, or refuses permission to the public to utilize it for fair compensation, it is admitted that society has a right to compel him to refrain from such neglect or abuse and to deprive him of the control of his property if he resists. This is done on general principles of utility, amounting in extreme cases to necessity. The modern State so interprets the maxim, *Salus republicae suprema lex,* as to interfere more and more with the rights of individual property, not merely in land but in other sorts, on the ground that certain exercises of these rights are not self-regarding actions but are social wrongs. In similar fashion, runs the argument, if a nation or the government of a nation holding possession of a piece of territory refuses to utilize fully its resources or to permit others to do so or otherwise makes itself a nuisance to its neighbors, or to the international public, the sacred rights of nationality ought not to protect it from coercion imposed on behalf of the general good of nations. The Transvaal, it is contended, was such a State; it would not develop its resources properly nor would it let others develop them; its backward civilization was a contamination and a menace to the States around it. The conquest and annexation of the Transvaal by Great Britain is justified on the ground that the world will be gainers by a just, settled and effective administration of the country and that Great Britain, as the nearest neighbor and as otherwise the power most competent for such a task, may regard herself as delegated by the civilized world to perform this task.

Now, with the general principle which underlies this argument no one but an individualist of the old school can quarrel. It cannot seriously be maintained that any group of inhabitants, by virtue of mere priority of occupation, or because they have for a certain time exercised government over a territory, would have a right (save perhaps in a strictly legal international sense) to neglect or abuse resources, the utilization of which might be an urgent need to the world at large. An extreme case rightly tests the issue. An inundation over the land of a nation causes it to be over-populated, or some persistent disease impairs its food supply, while beyond its national border lies rich land untilled and this by people belonging to some neighboring nation. An international court of equity would certainly accord to the people of the former State a right to use the land of the latter, and if necessary would enforce that right. If this holds in an extreme case, does it not hold of cases less extreme, where the need and the public utility of coercion are less?

This is clear. But let us see what is admitted. For the justification of such coercion we assume the existence of an International Court which represents the general good of nations, as distinct from the good of any particular nation; the right accorded to the needy nation is not a "natural" right but is international and rational in origin. To say that a nation, asserting its own needs in its own case without an express commission from the "international," has a right to apply, either on its own behalf or professedly for the general good, any such coercion, is to lapse into a national individualism which is as false as the individualism of absolute personal rights within the single nation.

Now, neither Great Britain nor any other imperial power, pleading "the general good" as a motive and result of its territorial aggressions, received a mandate or a sanction from any such International Court. In point of fact there exists no organized or recognized mode of expression of the general will of nations. So far as that will finds form in personal expression through diplomacy and the press, instead of sanctifying, it condemns each aggressive action of Great Britain,

Russia, Germany and America. It may, indeed, be a gain for world-civilization that Great Britain should annex the Boer Republics, Germany Strassburg, Russia Manchuria and so forth, but no recognition of this gain is given by Christendom which, as far as in it lies, condemns such acts as motived in each case by selfish greed and fraught with gain only to the aggressor. Though envy may bias judgment, there is no reason to doubt that the general sense of the civilized world regards our annexation in South Africa as wanton theft committed by a stronger power against a weaker, and nowise as designed to secure any general good.

To this it may be replied: "The fact that there exists no organized form of the reasonable expression of the international will must not deter Great Britain or any other nation from doing what she genuinely believes to be for the general good. If in any rude society regular processes of justice are not established, a man is justified in taking the law into his own hands; and his action must be judged upon the actual merits of the case. The admitted fact that the bias of personal interest will be present in such a case need not disqualify a man from punishing a wrong, or forcibly abating a nuisance, when no appeal is open to an impartial tribunal." So here it is asserted that we are justified in annexing the Boer Republics because this action, though repudiated and condemned by the current unorganized and irrational sentiment of other nations, makes really for the general good of nations. The fact that we make some particular national gain for ourselves, or avenge some particular national injury, though it may naturally rouse suspicions regarding the net result of annexation, must not be allowed to prevent recognition of the actual world-gain of this policy. The Boer Republics, passing from incompetent into competent administration, will in fact, by the sound development of their resources and the freedom of access and security of life and property afforded by the British flag, yield gains in which all nations must participate. "Such an action," it is maintained, "is really international, in that it helps to realize a truly enlightened world policy, the 'real' or rational will of the community of nations."

Here again the general reasoning, while it remains hypothetical, is impregnable; but its application is riddled by illicit particular assumptions. It is admitted that no act of aggressive imperialism is sanctioned by the direct expression of an international will. Can it be seriously maintained that consideration of the international gain, as distinguished from the selfish national gain, plays any considerable part as a motive in the policy of the expanding nation? Is it contended, in the particular instance of the Boer Republic that the good of any entity larger than the British Empire exercises any influence whatever in determining the act of annexation? The consideration that such wider good is consistent with, or incidental on, the pursuance of our selfish national end, though it is not present as a conscious determination of policy, surely borders on a region of most dangerous casuistry. If we are justified, in default of any constituted court of justice, in acting as judges in our own case, it is surely essential to show that some consideration transcending our own private gain, operates consciously in our minds as a standard of utility.

Before a stronger farmer, on a frontier where no regular justice is established, can rightly compel a neighboring farmer to adopt a more enlightened method of working and of living, and on his proving refractory, can shoot him down and seize his farm, a case of overwhelming strength must be made out, and, on his proving refractory, can shoot him down and seize ercing farmer will not be the sole gainer by his policy of force. Against a man or a nation acting as judge and executioner in its own cause there must always lie the onus of showing that it is not dominated, though it may be influenced, by purely self-regarding motives. It cannot be presumed that a course of action which is profitable to the stronger coercive nation will by some general process of international reactions prove profitable to the world in general, or that such profit, if it emerges, can safely be taken to overbalance the injury which such coercion always inflicts and which is graver where it appears, as it always does, to be the persecution of a weaker by a stronger nation.

The Utilitarianism which argues that because Egypt has

been a direct material gainer by our seizure of its government, that seizure was justified, though that gain was in no sense the directing motive of our seizure, is a short-sighted utilitarianism, because it ignores the utility of faith among nations, and the injury which the violation of distinct national pledges inflicts upon the moral relations between nations.

So, in the annexation of the Boer Republics, there is no evidence that we have been actuated in the policy by any consideration broader than a short-sighted calculation of British imperial interests, or that any broader interests are in fact likely to be subserved. The case for international good could hardly be weaker. The only material resources of the Transvaal which are known to exist were already in rapid course of development; nothing is gained by increasing the rate of output, nor indeed can it seriously be held that the occupation of capital and labor in these mining industries is a world-gain at all—it is rather a world-loss. Apart from the mines and the mining population it is not even pretended that any political issues would have arisen grave enough to warrant the expenditure of blood and money which has occurred, even from considerations of a purely British policy. It is difficult to show that even Great Britain will make any net industrial or political gain through annexation either on a short or a long range focus of utility: it is impossible to show that the transfer of power from the self-governing burghers to the British crown confers or will confer any general gain to the world, or that any slight industrial gain which might arise from more efficient development of the annexed countries will not be immediately outweighed by the cynical repudiation of our policy as it was defined at the outbreak of hostilities, and by the distrust and indignation which our conduct has aroused in every nation of the world.

The case of the South African War and Annexation is made still worse by the special circumstances. I have admitted that a nation may take justice into its own hands when no court of international justice exists, though it can only justify war and annexation by the clearest evidence of necessity. But in the South African business we have debarred ourselves from pleading that we are in reality the executive of a sound world-policy in pursuance of the general good of nations, by refusing to have recourse to a method of arbitration which, though not a perfect instrument of the general will of nations, is the best instrument available, and that upon our own recent admission. A Court of Arbitration for the determination of the whole issue might not have been constituted with absolute impartiality, but it must at any rate have been less partial than an appeal to the arbitrament of arms. The reason given for our refusal to arbitrate is conclusive against any pretence that our policy of imperial aggression is really designed for, or fraught with, the general good of the world. We refused to arbitrate on the ground that we had in the past forced upon the Transvaal terms of technical political inferiority. The Transvaal government disputed and denied the application of these terms: the issue resting upon the interpretation of written conventions. These conventions we refused to submit to a Court of Arbitration, although recently at The Hague we had expressly assented to a doctrine which assigned the interpretation of documents expressing international relations as a proper province of arbirtation. It is true that by making the exclusion of the Transvaal a condition of our entering the Conference, and by refusing the assent to the arbitration proposals, save on the condition that no outside powers could be admitted to their benefits without the unanimous sanction of the signatory powers, we had excluded the Transvaal from claiming arbitration as a technical right. But our assent to The Hague proposals is a complete admission of the ethics of the case, and carries precisely the same moral condemnation of our forceful policy, as if the Transvaal had been a full participant at the Conference. If any reader is disposed to evade the point by falling back upon the fact that the Boers opened hostilities, it is sufficient to remind him that the words used by the British representative at Pretoria some time before the war, "Her Majesty's government will, if necessary, press their demands by force," form an adequate statement of our intentions.

II.

It is a law of modern industry that the big business swallows up the smaller business, and that a number of small businesses coalesce in order to work more cheaply and more profitably: instead of a large number of little industrial units we find a smaller number of large units, and this process of combination or absorption proceeds until a few gigantic trade competitors find competition such a costly, wasteful thing that they decide to put an end to it by a culminating act of combination. This law, it is suggested, is likewise applicable to the business of government: small states federate or combine, big states swallow and absorb their smaller or weaker neighbors; a few big empires rapidly extend their areas, putting down the constant internecine struggles and substituting a rivalry of a few great political bodies which only indulge in occasional warfare, and which, in time, when the whole desirable territory of the earth is partitioned between them, will come to terms with one another and secure a peaceful federation of the world. This process is going on apace in the history of modern empires: each step of aggression or coercion may seem indefensible, but after all the absorption of smaller by larger states, of backward by civilized states, is an inevitable operation and makes for net economy in government. It is on the whole desirable that those nations who have best developed the arts of effective government shall extend the practice of those arts over the widest possible area. The larger an empire is the better and the more economically it can be administered, if due regard be paid to the special needs of provinces and districts under a properly devised form of local self-government with a system of central checks. It is entirely a matter of business organization, and the nation which shows most capacity for this work should undertake it. Great Britain, developing sound political methods, based on no vague abstract theories of government, but upon careful experience of all sorts and conditions of men, is able to find trained administrators of incorruptible honesty who shall ingraft these sound methods upon the new states which pass under her control. A capable and honest public service, equal justice for all men, greater security against external foes and intestine strife and more practical freedom of the individual than is found under any other government—such are the business advantages offered on the prospectus of Great Britain unlimited. Other civilized nations in proportion to their ability to apply the arts of government may participate, but since the Anglo-Saxon race has gone further and succeeded better than any other, it is well that she should do as much of it as possible.

The case of the Boer Republics is admirably to the point. Africa south of the Zambesi is physically and economically one country, the same race combinations occupy the different states, the same social and political problems present themselves for solution: a political federation of all these states is inevitable and desirable, it should take place under the British flag and the sooner the better. This political ideal, conceived by Lord Carnarvon more than twenty-five years ago, has now been realized by a later master-builder of the British empire.

Now this simple business view of imperial expansion is suspicious for its very simplicity, and when we see what it assumes on the one hand, and ignores on the other, the suspicion deepens into condemnation.

The big business analogy makes two assumptions, first that politics is rightly regarded as a business, secondly that it belongs to a class of businesses to which no limit of advantageous growth can be assigned. Let us take the second first. It is not true that there exists a law of general application in the economic world, according to which small businesses are swallowed by larger businesses and these again by larger still, the process terminating in a single giant business which secures industrial peace under the form of a private or public monopoly. In some trades, and in some branches of other trades, this law of economy by combination is operative until complete unity is attained. In many trades combination and growth of business form is attended by profitable economy up to a certain point, but beyond that point each increase of size and restraint of competition causes unwholesome corpulency with loss of vigor and capacity of progress. In many trades no such tendency is seen: businesses are small and numerous and remain so for sound reasons of economy. Of course, everywhere, certain economies attend growth in the size of business, but they are attended by certain causally related defects, and the net economy is different in every trade. Is government a business of which we can safely predict that every increase in its area is attended by greater economy and efficiency? In order to answer this question we must ask another: What is the essential character of the businesses which grow to the largest size with most advantage? The answer is quite clear: Adaptability to minute routine, to mechanical organization, for the supply of the common needs of large masses of consumers. To some it may seem that government in eminently a business of this order. Justice, security to person and property, and other protective services, which are the first chief objects of government are, it may appear, essentially of a routine character. In one sense this is true, in another false. The "commodities" supplied by the official classes who constitute the administrative side of government, justice, security, etc., are distinctively routine, conformable to rigid rules and of certain fixed sorts and sizes. Just in so far, therefore, as there exist tolerable homogeneity and constancy in the needs of citizens which these public commodities are designed to supply, do we get really efficient government: ideal justice, exact security, etc., are not obtained, but the official measures are fairly applicable. However big the area of a really homogeneous population might be, it is arguable that the area of government might so expand as to cover it, and perhaps even to develop increased efficiency and economy in doing so. What really limits the expansibility of a governmental area is that which limits the growth of a routine business, the necessity of satisfying the needs of heterogeneous and changing markets. The notion that there are certain common brands of "justice," "freedom," "civilization," which can profitably, or even possibly, be imposed upon widely divergent types of peoples so as to satisfy their needs, is a dangerous fallacy. The notion that even what are called "the elements of justice" are the same everywhere, and that therefore a just British civil servant can be safely trusted to satisfy the demands of justice in India or China, only survives on account of the inherent incapacity of English people for the study of psychology and the lack of imagination which disables them from understanding the psychical temperaments and valuations of other peoples. A British lawyer imposing British "elements of justice" in China would in every concrete case offend the ethical susceptibilities and violate the elementary sense of right in the best men of the Chinese community. It is, indeed, universally admitted, how utterly all European nations fail to understand that delicate multiform thing which is rudely generalized as "the Oriental mind." How then can we govern properly or "civilize" the owners of this mind? Routine methods of the big "governmental machine" are plainly incompetent to supply the elemental political needs of widely divergent bodies of consumers. We admit these when we apply measures of local self-government and endeavor to furnish elasticity to the machinery. But this very action serves to bring out the central fallacy. Devolution of power from a central government, always accompanied by forcible retention of a central veto, while complicating the mechanism of the single machine, does not confer that true freedom of local will that is essential to sound government of the "federal" type.

Not only is a definite limit set by considerations of efficiency and economy to the size of a single area of central government, but this limit cannot be got rid of by mere devolution from the centre, for that devolution is vitiated at the start by the arbitrary determination of the central power as to what subordinate powers shall be devoluted, and it is further vitiated by the temptation to overrule those very cases where the diverging will of the subordinate government is testimony to the radical defect of centralization.

This criticism implies not merely that government is not to be classed as one of the great routine businesses which grow stronger as they grow bigger, indefinitely, but that it is not rightly regarded as a business at all. Common parlance even dignifies it by the title Art. Now an art differs from a business precisely in the fact that its work is rightly dominated by considerations of the organic nature of man, the individual character of his wants and the necessity of applying individuality to procure their satisfaction. Just in proportion as government succeeds in being an art is it really successful. In order to be an artist an official must be in close knowledge and sympathy with the personality of the governed class. Now where there is great heterogeneity among the governed classes this is impossible; the attempt to make allowance for this heterogeniety only imparts more elaboration into the "machinery" of government and makes it more mechanical and so less capable of fulfilling the real functions of government. The extent and nature of this vice is hidden by the autocratic idea and temper which Empire commonly assumes and by a certain spurious temporary strength which emanates from military organization. The more Great Britain attempts to infuse Empire with Democracy, to implant, water and grow "free" institutions in her conquered states, the more glaringly apparent will become the contradictions between Empire and Democracy. Strong centralization based on and defended by Militarism may supply a powerful and tolerably effective machine for doing such inferior work as a machine can do, but attempt to "force" free institutions and British notions of self-government upon states whose native spirit we have crushed, and the failure will be evident.

This central vice of Empire is best shown by pointing out how the "business" view of economy of government ignores nationality. Our socialists who think it advantageous to break down the boundaries of nationalities, and force all men to become brothers, are not really the scientific gentlemen they claim to be. They want to substitute artificial catastrophe for natural growth. To them nationality is little better than a silly sentiment. If the Transvaal burgher can get better government under the British flag, more security against Kaffir incursions, better markets for their farm produce, and more even-handed justice, it is idle to let a sentiment stand in the way! The "business" man who "runs" British politics to-day naturally believes that a people who gain so much will soon settle down comfortably under the new form of government.

It is needless to point out how all "history" gives the lie to the business man by showing this sentiment as one of the most stubborn facts. But the case of the Boer Republics presents an even more important lesson. By breaking down the form of nationality in small peoples, and by seeking to break the spirit of it, we are destroying the most essential means of attaining in the future that solid federation of all civilized peoples which is the only hopeful security against the recrudescence of barbarism in the shape of war. As in certain parts of the ancient world there sprang up the City State, representing the best form of society then attainable, so our age is distinctively that of the Nation State, or, one may rightly add, the small nation-state. This is not a mere contradiction of the claims of Imperialism to represent the advanced civilization of Christendom. A candid consideration of the most valued essentials of social life will compel us to admit that the small European peoples such as Denmark, Holland and Belgium, Switzerland, Norway and Sweden, present more wholesome and progressive types of civilization, as we ourselves understand the thing, than any others, and that their smallness and their national self-concentration are chief conditions of this excellence.

The false economy of size which clings to the great autocratic empire (and every empire *quâ* empire is autocratic) conceals the true test of national greatness, the free effective expression and realization of the will of the people. That same quality of present nearness, neighborhood, which is the very essence of civic life, is also essential, though in a somewhat different way, to effective nationality. A militant Imperialism can cultivate and maintain a false form of *exclusive* nationalism which has its essence in hostility towards other nations, but a true *inclusive* nationalism demands the possibility of such personal relations among the members and classes of which a nation is composed, as shall yield a vigorous moral bond of sympathy. A small nation, with some approximate equality of economic and social conditions, can alone yield this moral basis of union. To imagine that the cause of an ideal internationalism can be promoted by breaking down the forms of nationalism and seeking to destroy its spirit in those little peoples where alone it truly thrives, is wholly to misunderstand the social problem. Internationalism is not the negation but the expansion of the national spirit. As sound civic forms and feelings are essential to strong nationalism, so sound national forms and feelings are essential to the slow gradual growth of an internationalism which shall develop for itself in due time valid laws and institutions. To maintain and foster the forms and spirit of inclusive nationalism in every state where they have taken firm root is the plain duty of every statesman who wishes to see grow up in the future true bonds of peace and brotherhood among nations. This is no idle speculation but verifiable hypothesis. Those best acquainted with the spirit and temper of the citizens of small states like Switzerland and Denmark will testify that life in these small democratic states, while stimulating an intense love of country, equally favors a tolerance of foreigners, a sympathetic interest in their affairs, and a desire to be on friendly terms with them and to learn from them. On the contrary, just in proportion as imperial habits and temper are manifested in the policy of a nation, and it develops territorial pride and expansive proclivities, goodwill towards foreigners diminishes, and definite antagonisms are set up. A comparison between Germany before the Franco-Prussian war and Germany to-day is convincing evidence. The forcible breaking down of small national boundaries, and the welding of huge empires out of the pieces, retards the process of world-civilization by crushing the external expression of the social nature of man in their largest and most valuable forms. The process of this mechanical coercion is bad, the result is worse. It substitutes for patriotism based on the mutual good will of countrymen an exclusive antagonistic "imperialism" based on force and finding its most appropriate expression in aggressive violence.

Our glory in the recent display of loyalty by the colonies of the British empire is the glory of blind folly. Do we call upon these children to love us, fend us, help us in our proper work, trusting by this common service in good doing to bind them closer to us? Not at all. We call upon them to help us hate our enemies and destroy them, to help us break down the constitutional liberties of two sister colonies and to found new colonies by forcing enemies to become British subjects. Will this experience really bind our colonies to us more closely in the lasting bonds of affection? Is confederacy in violence a sound pledge of friendship? Will the total union of colonies within our empire be really strengthened by making two new hostile colonies, and making secret foes of a majority of the subjects in another?

No! Unless politics are entirely a thing of paper constitution and of colored maps, these paths of Imperialism are not paths of peace leading to internationalism and world-civilization.

Nationalism is a necessary and a serviceable instrument of social growth. It has indeed no absolute validity or right that it should be respected where it is a grave scandal and danger to its neighbors or to civilization as a whole. But its utility is so great that nothing but the gravest urgency attested by the warrant of an impartial Court of Nations should justify the destruction of a nation and the annexation of its territory. Those who chatter about absorbing nations, as a big screw factory absorbs little ones, are either fools who know not what they say, or reckless politicians prepared to endanger the interests alike of the world and of their own nation to satisfy some lust of immediate self-aggrandizement.

The presumption must always hold that a nation in being is better adapted to its territorial environment than any other nation seeking to subjugate it, and should be left free to utilize its land and to grow its own political institutions.

Forcible aggression upon nationality strikes at the very root of civilization. Even were it true and determined by an impartial tribunal that the civilization of the conquering nation was better in kind or more advanced in degree than that of the conquered, this would not legitimatize such absorption. Either a nation, such as the Transvaal or China, is growing a radically different civilization with different arts of government from ours, or else such a nation is backward in the same course of civilization. In the one case it is impossible for us to civilize it, in the other "forcing" the pace is unwise and ultimately defeats its end by substituting artificial for natural progress.

The notions that the arts of government are portable commodities, that there is one best brand, the Anglo-Saxon, and that forcibly to fasten this upon as large a portion of the globe as possible makes for the civilization of the world, imply an utter misunderstanding of the very rudiments of social psychology.

That the attainment of anything which can be called a world-civilization involves some growing assimilation of national life, and even of forms of government between different nations, is obvious. Economists of two generations ago fondly dreamed that mutual trading interests and the intercommunication of men and ideas consequent on trade would secure rapid progress toward this goal. Wildly exaggerated as this dream may have been, it is not so manifestly chimerical as the dream of the new Imperialism that a forcible destruction of national barriers will advance the harmony of mankind. To substitute bonds of iron for the organic ligaments of international goodwill, and to pretend that this coercive process is sanctioned by laws of social evolution, is the grossest possible abuse of scientific method and of scientific terminology. A world federation of nations, in so far as it is ever possible, must proceed from the free will of enlightened nations approaching one another along voluntary paths of peace and goodwill. Such enlightenment is itself the latest and the choicest fruit of free nationalism. Every attempt to check this natural growth, or by force or menace to impose a policy, chills the atmosphere of national life and sterilizes the most promising seeds of the wider, saner nationalism which will seek to realize itself by cherishing the friendship of other nations, and coöperating with them for the attainment of the widest human ends.

JOHN A. HOBSON.

LONDON.

Milton Keynes UK
Ingram Content Group UK Ltd.
UKHW010635150124
436059UK00004B/406